HappyLand

HappyLand

A collection of new poems by Kim Hae-ja
Translated by Deborah Smith

K
POET
아시아

Contents

Flower of the moment	8
Erasure of the body	11
Neighbours	15
Nothing happened	19
Small Fry	24
Flock of birds of the subway train's floor	28
Moonlight Hologram	31
Red Spider Lily	39
Stone seaweed ear	43
Mask, 假面, 탈	47
Go-between	56
Happyland	60

Tarot Tower	69
Riding the upward escalator	73
Fable	76
Magnetic Resonance	82
Human being	87
Thinking feet	99
Over beneath the trees	103
Anonymous	109
Poet's Notes	114
Poet's Essay	132
What They Say About Kim Hae-ja	152

HAPPYLAND

POET

Flower of the moment

Your frozen feet crept under our quilt around dawn
Trying to thaw them, they liquefied, turning to tears and disappearing
Brimming droplets that sunk into my half-sleep
were the eyes of a god once met, since forgotten

Petals bloomed on snow from unearthed whispers,
white footprints revolving step by step
mandala that will always bloom again
you are the lips of eternity, always just-parted

In un-ageing time all 'firsts' live on a lease;

o, you are the moment frothing within dawn,

and you and I were a pair of naked urchins

swimming into time that was open on all sides,

foam flowers that frothed up together –

dreams fizzle out, sink back into the sea

and begin to build again

The horizon that recedes on approach

is the heel of the god I have never yet touched

O, bud of the moment that breaks on impact,

who can make tears bloom for other than love?

Stitch by stitch, side by side together,

white spume rising up

This now is always

a sweet-bitter fragment

that regenerates as though each time were the first.

O, you are a single sad spoonful of foam

breaking up again

Erasure of the body

Seriously, when I'm deadly depressed what I do is, I call a friend. Hmm, well, I turn the sound off, we'll both just say whatever we need to get off our chests and at some point we'll hang up, without the other realising...she can't hear what I'm saying and I don't know what she's saying. But I know she's there listening, you see. It stops me feeling like I'm all alone...you need social media too, any way to feel connected, the important thing is someone is giving me their attention, right...

Confided by a youth of almost 22, these words lingered a while after the lecture had finished, then followed me all the way to an alley in Namdaemun market. A bottle of soju just removed from the fridge sheds tears. Why do water droplets form on cold surfaces like glass bottles or beer cans? I couldn't ask. Did you really not want to know what they said? Did you really not want them to hear your words? I couldn't ask. Have something to eat. You need to line your stomach first if you're to take your fill of sadness.

Waking around dawn.
The sound of sob-choked coughing;
there is no one next to me The body remembers

words spoken to my 22-year-old self, even though you couldn't hear them

While we sang of it, love was coming to an immature end, and while shouting growth and progress, dejected cracks were appearing in the home. What? You want to live in an apartment? Ah, you want to buy one...while running from death sinkholes were yawning open in all directions, and while things both big and powerful were closing in, politics and groups of sharks, fragile lives were managing to flower in cracks of concrete, revolution was hitting rock bottom along with the stock market so economics, unproductive bodies, substructures that failed to be postmodern were said to have recently been relocated to a tumultuous black hole. How much does that cost, enough money to cover basic income for everyone on earth, that's how much. The broadening orbit meant everything grew gradually more distant, humanity has grown so vast, we're having to study a new language that's not even audible...wait, am I human? Ah, you really can't hear me...

The place where the body is erased
dense with unknowable radio waves.

Neighbours

After a month or so left empty

I enter hesitantly as though a guest in my own home; the woman from the house below, used to popping round whenever,

strides into the yard like it's hers,

hugs me, says it'll be okay,

somehow she knew I'd been far away, being ill, says not to worry,

we didn't let your radishes freeze, we pulled them up and made kimchi

and put the rest in a jar

Following the pointing finger and examining the

low wooden bench, old round pumpkins are resting against each other next to the bucket of young radish kimchi, a jar's interior packed with pale green radishes, radish tops are hanging from a low rope. Pii-ii-i chaek chaek, in the time it takes the chattering sparrows to hop from one branch to another the women from next door and the house opposite have also dropped by, it's as bustling as the village mill. White and green winter kimchi in a round stainless steel dish, ripe persimmons with a thin skin of ice, and the dried bricks of fermented soybeans at the house below all breathing together, each place my neighbours' hands have worked thriving is this hinge point after autumn's ending, with the first snows still to come

   Even when I leave this place

   and arrive in the other world,

   it seems my old neighbours, now forgotten,

   forgotten what with just getting by, will rush forward barefoot

   and embrace me swiftly like my own mother would,

   ah, my child, you must've had a time of it, having to come all this way,

   it seems they will pat me on the back

cheerfully mobbing me just like those sparrows

Nothing happened

I, sanding worker Jung Beom-sik, was discovered at 11.35am on 26th April 2014.

They said that I, described as a subcontracted labourer at Hyundai Heavy Industries in Ulsan,

was hanging from a 4m railing

with air hose #2626 from painting area #13 around my neck.

That morning, the remote control for the sanding machine I'd been using was playing up.

Each time I switched it to ON, the machine would throw out grit (metal dust) and then stop.

I'll give it one more go and if it's still not right I'll

have to fix it, I told a colleague.

When the contacts kept malfunctioning, I stopped my work

and hurried to the machine room via a scaffold at the far end of the block;

having taken my respirator mask off, wearing only a dust mask

I was in the middle of repairs when my face felt as though it was on fire.

In an instant the dust mask filter was torn off,

the sanding machine belched out grit, and I felt the force of it strike my upper body.

With metal dust embedded in my eyes,

I couldn't see in front of me.

Somehow I managed to crawl out of the machine room, and groped my way down the external scaffold, but the grit I was shedding made it slippery.

I called out, but there was no answer.

Leaning against the outer safety rail, I crawled towards the ladder.

As I moved to set my foot on its rung, I fell over the side.

The ladder I'd used to climb up

had been moved somewhere else in the meantime.

An air hose caught around me, tugged at me.

I was strangled.

The police and the company called it suicide.

I'd taken off my own hose and used someone else's to hang myself?

Me, who'd firmly taped up my shirt cuffs and waistband so the grit couldn't get in?

Me, who'd boasted about watching my daughter audition the day after next, strangled myself?

Me, who'd been out to buy cup noodles, and said we'd eat them together later – why? When the noodles were still uneaten.

The factory got off scot-free. I was just a suicide.

Nothing happened.

Small Fry

A box of large anchovies pours onto newspaper –

hundreds of eyeballs looking up at me

Scattered across the faces of old-time government officials

the anchovies were ready to be sorted and trimmed

when my daughter drew back, asked

Mum, are those eyes looking at me?

With backs split open and heads torn off

the insides ripped out, that fishy odour

Eyes that stare open in severed heads,

eyes that are looking at those eyes,

the question once put from a careful distance

doesn't get asked anymore.

Wordless as anchovies, line lunchboxes with your daily sustenance

Those wordless things bulked up a meagre meal of stir-fried kimchi and pickled radish

Those close-mouthed heads gave savour to poor fare of white radish and green onion

Anchovies crushed into a crunchy powder

Not rich tuna or plump yellowtail

Delicate sea bass or meaty salmon

These small silver bodies each become the strong bones

of miner, lathe-worker, and farmer,

in bent knees, the joints of their fingers grasping

pick-axe, welding machine, and hoe;

like fishers who shake anchovy nets with a soft uh-sha

delivery workers who leave boxes by doors without a word

plantain straightening its neck again after getting trodden down

silk grass, mung bean grass drawing barely any attention

these nothings

these small fry gather

Flock of birds of the subway train's floor

Heading home on the quiet subway for the first
time in a while
I was staring at my feet when I came to realise
that a sea was flowing there;
spume of waves spurting up, shattering,
stars littering the pale blue floor

The closer I looked, glittering points of land stars
became silver birds flying through that blue.
Heading back, mouths full with what
will be put in their babies' chirping, gaping beaks
the birds do not speak. Worn out and broken
down,

wings beating against the floor

Residents of an out-of-the-way nook of the galaxy, we came to put in a shift in this solar system which takes two hundred million light years to turn once around the galactic centre; a cosmic millstone turning and turning without rest, a chip off time turning under its own volition, each day following the course of the zodiac, the moon pulls milk through pale nipples and putting my lips to them I flounder, swelling up and bracing myself and bouncing around, flying across the floor

The stars' bodies bear indelible wounds.

The marks of struggles to keep one's footing while shoving and being shoved together, being shaken side to side

silver points, points flying together
at level height across the squared-off floor

Moonlight Hologram

0

Thick fog swaddles the mountain's midpoint,

an auspicious serpent whitely wriggling,

the sea laps at the roof of my friend Deoksim's house

and the moon is in the water. There are times when dreams are more realistic

than any waking state.

When the moon rose swollen,

drops of milk trickled through your flesh

Plump fish leapt above the waves, a cheering crowd,

hands raised, balancing on slender ankles

As you came closer, I disappeared

Goggle-eyed gobies used their wings to jump and yellowfin gobies rolled on the mudflat

and mud crabs bloomed bubbleflowers, slowly crawling

to the silver-powder-saturated-sea

Wriggling in your arms, we touched as I fed

and we were a dance vibrating to the rhythm you set

Yesterday and the day before, last year and the year before, the sun rose and set just the same

and among paddy fields that raise rice plants in rainwater, a white expanse stretching down to the sea,

was a village of feet treading wooden wheels, like walking up a moving stairway, slowly,

milling salt grains through steps that never alter

A border of light to the black night

when the moon was cold and slanting,

birthing fish as it pushed and pulled at the sea

A single point inside the big bang that nibbled away at it in play

We were too close to each other

to know that you are I are separate

Just as the you I'd exchanged blows with in the dream

was an avatar I'd made

1

It came from across the water; The modernisation of the motherland

brought with it the holy cross and competent English,

with factories and suits and engineers, tailcoats concealing weapons;

with the peddlers of Enlightenment in tow, stuffed

with learning

on how to better oneself, only better oneself

Children left on boats before they even came of age

We who were born in this land are charged with the historic mission of national restoration.*

picking the National Education Charter

off palms that were caned when they couldn't memorise its lines,

to work as babysitters, housemaids, in distant fac-

---

* from the National Education Charter, as promulgated by President Park Chung-hee on 5th December 1968, which we had to memorise from elementary school onward.

tories

I realise that the prosperity of the nation is the foundation of my own development.*

My cousin who I once fell asleep with playing in a straw rick on Daeboreum,

got one arm eaten up in a printing press

and like my father's cousin who came back with a metal arm in his shabby military jacket

lay prone on the salt flat flapping one arm

The spirit of our ancestors is revived today.*

Like fingers tightly grasping a spoon, so as not to

miss the meal

    my friend whose head used to touch the leaves

    when it was their turn to jump over the rope

    beneath the zelkova trees in Jeonggak pavilion,

    came back only after their lungs were worn out

    Setting white liquid flowing and birthing fish,

    the moon amid darkness

    monthly salary – monthly rent – monthly instalment – month-end tax adjustment

    we'd grown too bright to see your shadowed self

    and when you had grown slender as a sheet of paper

no longer sad, we burned ourselves to ash; we became adults,

became labourers; forgot kisses; grew half-dead with fatigue

Red Spider Lily

In the calendar of my native peninsula each day is the day of a patriotic martyr

There is no day a memorial service cannot be held

No day the requiem is not sung

10.1

10.2

10.3

even if not crape myrtle if not autumn leaves

still there is no path not stained by some

red flowerwater, petals torn to pulp

The history of my native land comes through keenly felt numbers

3.1

4.3

4.16

even if not azaleas if not camellias

there is no mountain-river-scape not dyed by a bloody sunset

O stripped-bare book of my homeland, each page turns

with a gut-wrenching sound

4.19

5.18

6.25

O red spider lily colony, bloomed from bullets embedded

  in the abdomens of those crazed with hunger

  They died out, they say, before seeds had time to form?

  No

  it's only since those flowers fell in a flurry

  that green stems pushed up in a flush

  The future of flowers

  that will be cut away and buried and still sprout again

  Love was shared; naked bodies embraced and

brought forth young; and they were suckled;

blood washed; blazing forth

from a dark cave frozen underground

a tongue of fire

was nurtured.

Stone seaweed ear

As soon as the thick ears of seaweed meet the brass bowl of water, they wriggle. Stiff layers fused together slacken apart, and slippery sap seeps out. They uncurl outwards, elder sister I've got your seaweed sorted, one bundle of seaweed with ears stuck huddled like barnacles comes bearing the voice of Kim Jong-bok from faraway Geomundo, followed by mum's, a-ya, I've already asked for some to be sent from Uido... three days of agony I had to go through when I had you... that tinglingly cold midnight at the year's end... ayaya it was grim as hell, her Jang-heung dialect slips and slides, the old hill by the coast spreads saltily aya, it's only the kind that grows where it's scarily deep that has ears, you know

 panting of mums spawning eggs in their ears until their whole bodies blue

 fanning of fin-flapping dads holding bubbles in their mouths

 the moment the mucosal iron-salt song stops and we stare

 the sound of silence collecting

Incheon Shinhyeon-dong Sandong-ne, where the wind blew through the building and the room was more like a box, a snug fit if there'd have been two

of me, the walls rustle. Too pregnant to lie on her
back or side, a woman munches on long strands of
seaweed. Ears open up between dried anchovies and
seasoned seaweed, that sped here with mum all the
long way from Mokpo harbour to Incheon harbour.
Saltily spreading sweetness rustles on newspaper
~ swi-u, swi-u, the sound of breath-rain spouting
from living mouths of Jeju divers ~ an airhole opens
in the abyss, and amniotic fluid undulates in suit ~
due any day now, in the belly of a woman who has
neither savings account nor medical insurance, the
baby kicks.

Dried stone seaweed ear

I've become hard of hearing;

the deep sea that lies far, far away over the mountains, I don't hear it so well any more.

Ears that cling to life by sticking together,

the march of musical notes that seep out

each time an ear uncurls

between one note and another

between in-breath and out

wave dash ~ you

as though hearing the breathing of you all

the sticky sea forms droplets

Mask, 假面, 탈
- Corona 1

Walking through the park; the person coming

from the opposite direction

stands aside to let me pass.

They cover their mouth courteously,

even their dog on its lead is waiting obediently

for me to hurry past;

the human race's long-held habit

of moving the shortest distance towards their goal

is breaking down

With nose and mouth covered,

everything below the eyes,

what refined animals we've become, maintaining a

distance

   between one person and another;

   preferring personal routes and detours

   we've become a new sapiens;

   having learned how to wait at a distance

   with head quietly lowered

   rather than staring each other in the face –

   what a composed, civil species is being birthed

2

The whole world

seems to have stopped kissing.

Fear has conquered love!

A small thing has conquered a big one!
Something invisible like a virus
is pushing away the person next to me

We no longer encounter each other.
Even those tender gazes have stopped,
where the whole body seems dipped in the other's eyes

Even when we used to look at each other
some things always did go unseen,
but as soon as you mask faces whose nakedness
used to mean equality between us,

we became a race of tranquil meditators.

Unable even to shout

a furious back off!

or seal an I love you with our saliva

3

When was it, when we last ate as a hubbub crowd,

guffawing together, our lips flecked with spit?

A medallion fritter of egg-dipped meat, the moon's

flat disc trembles the leaves.

The sound of chopsticks clicking,

poised in mid-air,

   placing courgette fritters and mung bean pancake on top of rice,

   the sound of doenjang soup bubbling

   somewhere far off,

   green onion buoyed up on pumpkin slices, mushrooms draped over tofu chunks,

   and diligent spoons dipping into the ddukbaegi.

Beneath the full moon a bonfire is burning.

Young and old, women and men are gathering.

In the yard where grain stalks are stacked on Daeboreum the sound of Gang-gang-sul-rae

   danced in a circle holding hands

ching ching ching ching, striking the gong until it leaves a mark,

the sound is rippling out in widening circles.

The opium eater, the consumptive, the beggar who was such a lively dancer,

even the taffy seller whose scissors were like music to the ears are gathering.

Shredded radish and beansprouts and seasoned bracken bellflowers sweet potato stalks

and cabbage and dried radish leaves, people coming together like that

Under the broad moon we're all in this thing together.

Metallic laughters mixing.

4

The tall pine who lacks a fellow tree to lean on

pricks the moon with its machine-sharp needles.

A viscous sentence slides out and down,

a silver spoon printed clumsily on copper-coloured

paper.

O foreign machinist making masks in dust

that makes your nose stream with mucus and pus,

so you too wear a mask

and block your nostrils with shreds of tissue,

you whose spine and legs are getting twisted

from 12 hours a day hunched over the machine,

look down at the treadle

Blocked-up mouth of stones

You who pour molten metal into the furnace, heat up the tomb

where rampant cold and hunger have been rounded up,

locked away, buried alive

Dry them out,

the poor people and worn-out clothes, buried alive and seething like mould

Dry the porcelain bowls containing coughs

covered over and bound with stinking silence

Miner mining the bitter abyss,

unknown children not yet born

clothed in the heart of a youthful sun,

the warm ground of the future

kiss it now

Go-between
- Corona 2

Told to sit tight at home as I have an existing medical condition, I heard

Geomundo National Federation of Fisheries Cooperative Go-between #35 Choi Hyung-ran

wants to send me some fish from that distant island, two hours by boat from Yeosu,

so I texted her the addresses of some juniors in Daegu

Salted whole mackerel and mackerel chunks come to land again after crossing their home the sea,

Such a generous serving, and so nicely presented, with this vigorous praise several pairs went to my elderly mother and two or three were sent on to friends

I received a job lot of vaccine, so I'll eat well and get my strength up

Kim Byeong-ho who packs and delivers gimbap called to tell me,

giving his news also to my neighbours

even the trees, the water deer and the stars

Three days later, Choi Hyung-ran called to say the women's association

wanted to chip in, contributing 8 large crates of fish.

Four days after that, dried and whole cutlassfish, attractive Japanese Spanish mackerel
 arrived at Daegu Fool's Tavern where Kim was packing gimbap
 to feed medical workers and other adults now cooped up in cramped rooms

There's so much...what is this grace...
 they shared it out and shared it out again,
 Kim Ch'ae-won who shared it out, the broker Choi Hyung-ran
 teared up, as did I, an unplanned go-between.
 Did even the miracle of the loaves and fishes do so

much?

Sharing is all we need in this life.

Happyland

Red Boots A pair on the feet of a pole bearing cumulus clouds. 9pm, red boots descend and two small feet are slipped in. A lamp above your red hat shining bright as the full moon, carrying a bamboo bag and metal skewer Red Boots goes up the mountain. Bantar Gebang* grows higher each day, you have to rummage through the rubbish heap if you want to find the treasure. Each place Red Boots steps there's hidden paper and plastic, tin cans are the best treasure, and the water bottle you're drinking from now you mustn't throw away somewhere

---

* Bantar Gebang: Indonesia's largest landfill site, where an average of 7,000 tons of rubbish is piled up every day from Jakarta and surrounding towns

else, avoiding the excavator you cut yourself on some glass. Blood flows down over the trainers. Binding the wound with a handkerchief, Red Boots resumes the treasure hunt. Next to, underneath, big blue boots tumble all around. They seem to have been scattered by a television falling from the excavator, such a small hydraulic shovel is nothing to be scared of,

3 in the morning, Red Boots returns to the mud hut. After two hours' sleep it's time to head to school. Even after all the scrubbing, the smell of rubbish remains. I am Nadia, 11 years old, I'm sad because my friends don't sit next to me, at school

we read the Quran. I can't read the Quran so the teacher got angry. Why is god unfair to me, little 神, Red Boots slumps over the desk and cries

Street dancers 8, 9, 10, and 11 years old, the 5 Eagle Brothers who met on the streets, sleep and work in the streets, go to buy a sack as soon as the sun comes up. They scavenge food and plastic bottles from among the rubbish of Happyland*, who knows where it comes from. A glass bottle is embraced as though it's a jewel. Nimble as dancers, they bend to

---

* A place on the coast in the Philippines where 60,000 people pushed out by urban development live

pluck out sweet-smelling cake paper and chocolate wrappers. Actual food avoids these ragged urchins, just like kids in cute dresses and smart uniforms do. Scram! A broom cracks Eagle Brother #5 on his back.

370 won for 1kg, 500 won in 7 hours, 7 hours of groping and you share bread bought by rubbish translated into money. It rains. Cardboard boxes and Styrofoam beds get shifted around. The more they shudder in the rain the more it soaks them with dreams, and though the 5 brothers cannot even dream of getting enough to eat, they do dream of earning money to help poor people. They dream

of becoming a firefighter, or an architect who builds homes for those who don't have any, the dreams of these dancers get drenched in the rain that lashes mercilessly down.

Jumper boy Happyland filled with floating matter, the seas around holiday condos are where 13-year-old Mick works, scavenging plastic. The cold sea spray gives him goose bumps. Balancing on a Styrofoam board, he fishes out floating plastic bottles. They'll only take water bottles if they're clean, will give only scrap metal money, recyclables gathered over several days made 40 pesos, which bought him one sausage and two sacks of rice. Taking the sausage to eat with his rice, their father says he is trying hard to find work, to not go hungry, dad used to work at the docks but now he's a professional boozer. When will you give me money for alcohol? He drinks again so as to forget. If you keep jumping up onto the trucks you'll die, your life will end,

Asphalt obscured in front with dust, he keeps an eye out from his perch on the railing of the bridge; he's like an eagle intent on potential prey. There's a truck going slow; it's a truck; let's go, Mick immediately breaks into a run and jumps up onto the truck. He rips out the steel frame and tosses it from the truck bed. Francis comes too, a younger boy from the neighbourhood who treats Mick like an elder brother. 7-year-old Francis, who envies squirrel-swift Mick, dreams of growing up quick to become a jumper boy, First you jump to grab the side of the truck, then you scramble up, you gotta keep moving, young Francis gives Mick a thumbs up.

Let's sell it and get something to eat, and go on a computer, a little over 1kg of wire has made him a rich man. Bro, what will happen if we fall from the truck? The cars don't stop, so if we fall we die, of course

Young saints I will cross the sea today, in the open-air yard of Manila harbour there are many rusty nails, they have to swim water 1.5km in depth, Francis is too small to keep up with Mick. I have to beat the older boys to it, two hours it takes Mick to swim to the harbour, and when he does he finds Francis has followed him there. Envy won out over fear. It hurts, I cut myself on a nail, there's blood, there are more wounds on his hands and feet than nails collected. Bro, I'm thirsty. Hunger wins out over pain. They climb a tree, pick some red fruit and eat. Mick's wish is to become a truck driver. His other wish, to be a good father. Francis' other wish, aside from becoming a jumper boy, is not to go hungry, to eat lots of delicious things,

  Swimming back across the wide stretch of sea
  the two do not speak
  Today we barely earned anything,
  just 24 pesos, so let's split it 12 each
  Touching the coins that have been placed in his hand, Francis* laughed like the saint.

---

* Francis passed away from a severe fever before he was 8 years old. (EBS documentary Children of Heaven).

Tarot Tower
- Corona 3

One foot on the water one on the green earth

treading softly

the archangel Michael, golden-winged,

pours water from one cup to another

In that moment, I left the #14 forest path where hyacinths had bloomed underfoot,

bound in the Devil's chains,

and came past the greedy #15 main road

Sparks are flying from the tower rearing up on the cliff,

in a corner of Scorpio the gods' home is on fire

and lightning strikes in gusting storm clouds;

bearing cracks like forked lightning, time is falling,

the collapsing tower, its hat –

its crown – all are falling upside down

A refugee camp,

a temporary place of shelter from bullets,

the tower tumbles, and we both are falling, you once alive and I not undead

The living dead who must die to live

find freedom and abundance in death

At night when the sun goes out,

you have to bury the scores of dead and take the road to #17;

bearing your many wounds

Water flows free from the bottle, wetting the spring and the wood;

star woman sprinkles the dry earth,

behind her naked body the Big Dipper surrounds the North Star;

before long the newborn moon will drop golden petals formed from tears,

crawfish and crab will crawl out of the water,

and beneath the yellow sun a child wearing a red cape,

riding a foal, back to the wall,

will set out on a long journey;

the surviving sunflowers and dead wall will see the child off;

hearing the trumpet blast rousing the morning, get up!, underwater

children will open their caskets

and reach out their hands

Riding the upward escalator
- Corona 4

36.5 degrees,

said the youth in protective clothing who had applied

the thermometer to my left temple. A sigh of relief

puffed my speechless mask.

Riding the hospital escalator up, knowing only how to go up

and not down,

I thought of the temperature of the Earth, this huge ark.

The rainforests are on fire

California is burning and Australia is burning.

While Amazon is thriving, indigenous peoples are being stretchered out

While Coupang is booming, workers are dropping dead

While Monsanto is expanding, peasants are going blind

Trees and grass are burning and koalas are burning Guiltless

kangaroos are writhing Clutching our young offspring

you and I are divided The earth's body and people's,

the Solomon Islands, Micronesia are disappearing

Tuvalu and Palau, Papua New Guinea are becoming submerged,

Incheon harbour and Incheon airport float on that water We are rescuing each other

from the ship we are trapped inside My gagged breath is panting

'Let's go get a bite to eat sometime,'

that common, casual statement of intent now has no certainty of coming to pass

Distance doesn't lessen the hurt

I miss even those I've not yet met

Fable

   From the cracks in the concrete in front of the basement one-room
   henbit raises its head; pressed down by smashed bricks
   shepherd's purse spreads its leaves, and green moss grows
   even on the half-uprooted, listing tree; I don't know
   the solidarity of seeds and water droplets that flowed underground last winter,
   your secret that shot up above the earth

   Vertical lines colonise the horizon,

things like enormous steeples, places of worship re-manufacture forged beliefs

and schools inject square knowledge, into those who crawl in lines like ants,

weapons guard imprisoned justice, immovable institutions propagandise idols,

the World Bank prints dollars,

and while the nation trapped inside the building shouts growth and development

farmers get ignored in the push for agriculture, workers are less important than factories

The tree withers to death unless its roots are

packed thick into the earth;

progressiveness gets uprooted unless it's knitted tight into the chest;

activists are made to surrender unless they extend a bridge to the masses;

in the march of mad fetishists who cannot see beyond statistics

in the balance sheet in the computer that gets called civilisation

I doubt, therefore I am

Cracks formed in the cement we put our faith in

of this faith only bones now remain

the pious glass wall shatters and the employees walk out;

in the mirror of faith which has no thickness, only length

Bipedalism came before the brain;

evolution began from the feet;

human hands are what lend heat to life, not the fable known as the system

Hands walk out of school buildings, grasping frying pan, drill, and brush

grassroots walk out from inside the nation; at best

stealing or stooping to pick up scattered cardboard boxes,
those who exist outside of documents
which know nothing of rot, of toughing it out

The tall tree sticks to the brusque rock
muddy clumps of soil cling to its roots
mud, vegetation's undergarments
sometimes roots become stairs, and walking on them we rise;
mud and trees, even uprooted, are a home for insects and moss – these are my religion

Knees squeeze the windpipe; with my voice lost

I resist, therefore I exist

Magnetic Resonance

It was a little like the sound of teeth grinding

And also like that of bone being sawn in two;

a wheel screeching over a bump, a truly terrific din

Magnetic resonance machine MRI,

the world shouting from inside a sealed casket

as though all of its yells were replayed one by one

Flat on my front

my chest juddered where it touched the hollow tube.

Help me, please help me, get me out of here for god's sake,

and I came so close to pressing

the jiggling lifeline, sole connection to the outside world;

the final emergency bell

attached to the end of the tube,

a ball like the globe we live on

and while I wavered over whether to push it or not

it's called magnetic resonance,

so might the sound be a sound-tattoo inked into my body,

in other words, the sound of let's go here no let's

go there at a loss

    this is correct that is correct pushing and pulling;

    how many mes can there be, that it's still not done

    inside the invisible

    magnetic field

    of numerous parts where the resonance is ongoing

    I began to ask

    Who are you?

    to each separate and individual sound

    turned out of the nooks and crannies inside me,

to the only world there is, which I had mistaken

for 'outside'

Baby, where is your home?

to the white pebble I cast away, done with playing,

to the smooth tombstone and withered cotton-

grass

Before I knew it, friendly

prickly mouths came hobbling out of the bright

light

Barley ears my friends and I grilled and ate on a

spring day, giggling,

   their pale green grains pushing outside the leaves

   Baby, what are you really?

Human being

Midwinter, Capricorn

So Ho-soon came to see me.

Mum of a close friend of forty years, whose table I'd been a frequent guest at

since being a twenty-year old prepping to retake the university entrance exam, she strode briskly in.

Her backpack, sweaty from toiling up the steep hill,

disgorged an endless stream of packages: fresh and long-fermented kimchi, soy-braised beef,

and my special favourites, green onion kimchi and salted octopus,

brilliantly golden pumpkin soup

Omma, what're you doing omma, where are you omma, incessantly calling like this

it seemed my long-departed mother had returned to me alive.

My appetite kicked in.

Omma So Ho-soon bustled about with scourer, dust cloth, dish towel in her hand, a demon for dust,

made sure the house was spotless,

then announced I'm going, and left.

Barely a fortnight after my post-op discharge.

Still winter, Aquarius

Early morning before breakfast there was a knock

at the door.

The auntie from the house below was standing there with a pot of soup.

Round yellow taro bobbed like birds' eggs in the liquid.

Yukkaejang. She said to wait a minute,

and returned with a pot of sticky rice, studded with jujube and gingko nuts and chestnuts and red beans

Two neat dish cloths were draped over the edges of the pot.

My next door unni came with pickled radish, pickled cucumber, sea lettuce in chilli sauce,

pushing a sealed cart containing tubs of kimchi she'd made for me.

The smell of the magic marker

that had drawn a plumb line from my throat to the pit of my stomach,

a horizontal line between both armpits, to form a cross in the centre of my chest,

making graph paper of my naked body

over which a galaxy had seemed to rotate

still lingered ten days after I'd come back

from thirty rounds of radiotherapy.

Hinging into spring, Pisces

When I groaned in the middle of the night, those who fetched a damp cloth

to wet my mouth and cool my forehead,

and smiled to hide the concern that threatened to leak out,

were those with neither home nor temple. When I was thrown out,

those who took me in and put me up

were those who didn't have much going for them.

A manhwa shop owner or a construction worker living in short-term rentals,

those who only deal in small change, they were superheroes to me.

Those who fed me when I was hungry were those who don't read

thick books like the Buddhist code or the Bible.

They were those who cannot read.

Poverty and illiteracy, my master.

Their hands and feet were prayers and books.

They were the sky and rice and poetry.

Finally spring, Aries

It was the time for flag raising Again

they were rising up

straight as warriors Saplings were soaring

higher every day.

I found them this morning on the pots outside –

red chilli leaves, kalopanax shoots, Siberian ginseng, ailanthus shoots, all gathered from the woods

I didn't know who had left them there. The heavens I don't know

will be as many as the seeds hidden in manure. I encountered heaven in the course of my life,

so there was nothing more to seek.

I am a human being, there is no need to fly off anywhere.

I live as a human being As a human being I will die

Summer is coming, Gemini

One afternoon when a light sprinkling of rain had fallen

I turned over the earth, crouched over like a hoe.

Grass had pushed up through the soil overnight.

I dug up goosefoot Between the roots, earthworms tunnelled slender paths through the soil.

I tore up thorny Japanese hop;

the sound of laughter tumbled over the climbing rose wall.

My friend's yard is like the village mill today,

That one crouches all day just to make the grass grow,

laughter rises and spreads in the air,

drifting over the wall and past me as I roll around in the dirt,

keeping time with the murmuring voices of the one-time babes in arms, one-time

girls who would have hurried back into the house when called

Jeongin-ah, Seungbun-ah, Taeyeol-ah

one-time young ladies who used to bow their heads modestly when called

Yeongja-ssi, Geumrye-ssi, Yeonggu-ssi, Yeonghee-ssi, Jeonghee-ssi Misook-sii

above prettily plaited hair

the whistling of pigtail bachelors.

Years that seem mere hours ago

are rising and spreading in the clear air.

No strongman is a match for midsummer grass,

the curved hoe supplied the mill belt with a handful of word-saturated soil.

Each time I flexed my waist with a grunt and tugged one up, right on cue

came a gust of wind. Pink moon-viewing flowers

broke through last winter's reed matting and soared up.

I was merely

mighty grass.

Each fluttering, gleaming, twirling leaf

on a single Suwon poplar.

Human being, whose past and present are both in

the progressive tense

Being Being Human Being,

the tune sounded further away, then closer.

Bing, bing, bing...

Spacetime filled with silence,

soil caved in to form a hieroglyph

doom doom doom...

they were caressing

embryos that had just opened their eyes,

their curled fingers

Thinking feet

Feet, the aunty from the house in front called them,

roots like centipede feet sprouting densely from the bottom of the garlic,

white garlic roots neatly lined up,

as she peeled the tooth-like cloves with the foot-like roots.

The Earth was a home. Small springs and small hills

and waterfalls that shatter into hundreds of branches

were each a home.

For human beings, too, there were trees that had a single root.

A tree of life, stretching out branches here and there,

made leaves sprout and flowers bloom, gave birds and insects a place to lodge.

Feet came five million years quicker than the brain.

Homo floresiensis, called 'Hobbit', both dependants and spirits of the forest,

had as much brain as the chimpanzees they split off from, but died out 50,000 years ago.

The appearance on earth of peoples who mix with other species and make fire happened one million years ago, but

walking on two legs came five million before that.

Even small-brained homo habilis used stone tools two million years ago.

We thought to the extent that we walked, and evolved to the extent that we thought.

Only by going walking could we encounter, shake hands, embrace.

We revived. Even without the strength to stand up walking revives the past, makes the future visible, awakens the now.

  Feet see the smallest flowers stuck to the ground

  The way feet think can never not be down to earth.

Invisible to the naked eye,

  unborn multitudes twitch their brains.

Like two sticks,

two bare trees, the 11th month

peels off the year that precedes it.

In walking forward, one year births the next.

  Footed garlic selves have already reached the garlic patch.

Over beneath the trees
- in memory of Kim Jong-ch'eol

My Father has passed away. Our heavenly father, everyone's big brother, who introduced himself to juniors, has passed away.

His shoes cost 30,000 won;

plain-living and benevolent, a friend to us all,

who ran hop-skip through the streets like a child, wearing shoes so old the colour had faded, because, he said, they were just so comfortable;

my friend who would stand me dinner and drinks every other month, tell me not to act cool, the comrade who lived by his own example – taking an interest in other people and doing what he could for them – has passed away; the teacher whose reproofs stung as his hugs sustained,

  who would always ask after those struggling and in pain, and stood by them,

  a friend to the earth, who toasted peasants, rural villages, and small farmers, has passed away.

  Invisible crown, corona

  in the whirlpool where the world tumbles down towards death

  tinnitus, the screech of airplane wheels that never let up,

  it is a ringing in the ears where not only the head and chest but the whole body of the earth is screaming,

    we just have to grit our teeth and start to hope,

    friend of water and trees and the earth and the wretched

    who cried out with all their soul in the wilderness

    Don't laugh don't cry, the Himalayas' head is breaking up

    and the Alps' chest is breaking loose

    Don't cry don't laugh don't cry for me,

    bloody tears stream out of Antarctic glaciers,

    and Siberia is on fire. Even if through gritted teeth, still, cry for burning Siberia,

lament for those torn apart by greed,

That 25th of June when winter set in overnight

under the zelkova tree I see

that the tree's capillaries are plunging desperately

downwards

to the rice paddy, its head jammed into the earth,

performing a handstand;

Father's book

〈Green Review〉*

One year, two years,

ten years, twenty years, twenty-nine years

until a single seed became a thousand individual fan-rib shadows

feeding on rain and snow and sunlight, the pattern of time forming within lightning at times,

---

* 〈Green Review〉 was published and funded by Kim Jong-ch'eol as a bimonthly magazine over 29 years from November 1991 without missing an issue. Its 173 issues practiced and were directed towards an ecological civilisation that goes beyond symbiosis and enjoyment and modern civilisation, while presenting realistic proposals for local currency, basic income, citizens' assemblies etc, based on current circumstances and which combined democracy, ecology, small-scale farming, and cooperative self-government. 〈Green Review〉 was known as the only magazine in the world with reading groups, of which there are more than 30. Kim Jong-ch'eol passed away suddenly on the morning of 25th June 2020.

a shard of hope written down with the feet

what a shame it would be, to leave this world to die out.

Living words are thrown stones,

radiating out until the universe is no more.

We are going to hear – words that are one body

with the sound of the earth's breathing

We are going to see – the invisible hand

of a man who was a friend to us all,

setting bow to string

behind the resonant notes

Anonymous

Artificial even in name, Artificial Intelligence Hospital floor 12,

even the lines of rain in the air are artificial, so the sound of it in the corridor

seemed liquid falling from the drip in my forearm.

The face of the poet who fell to their death from a tall building

and had spent their whole life engaged in manual labour

seemed a ghost glimpsed in the glass window, tearing branches off a tree,

wet motorbikes and cars waiting at a red light,

scattered glimpses of the other world.

Unable to lie down or sit,

the time when the heart is pumping furiously,

the needle shows the pressure rise above 180mmHg

poetry flows from my mouth like a moan

that in-transit hour of flying through the rain,

I ran. Horse of the blue dawn

holding one golden rein,

what might lie between earth and sky?

That slender line not even 1cm in length,

that ate up life's time, ever hungry,

shorter than the gash that opened on my little toe-nail

when the glass dish fell from the fridge –

1962.1.17 –

What will come after it, I do not know;

I won't know until the moment comes for me to go;

I won't know even after I've gone.

This now, when unfinished tomorrow is,

between a single point,

becoming yesterday,

I was holding my own funeral. I opened my eyes.

Anonymity determines me. I am getting erased, and

ignorance and darkness are birthing me.

Forgive me,

I said too much about too few things, about myself.*

---

* from Paul Celan's No one's Rose, "I said too little / about too many things, about you"

POET'S NOTES

Happyland borne in an ark

Invisible crown, corona: We cannot meet up with other people. A world I never experienced before is unfolding in front of me. People back away to avoid others, keeping their distance. It seems the whole world has stopped kissing. That we used to get together to eat and laugh and be rowdy seems like a miracle. Our faces' nakedness was the only way we were equal, but there is something unsightly about them now, more than half covered up. If it's only a casual acquaintance, I fail to recognise them. And even if we're ill, we seem in good health. Lilies wearing spray masks on their feet are looking under those feet with suspicion. Motorcyclists, who even have masks on their helmets, are racing up steep alleyways. I seem to glimpse birds wearing medical masks on their tails and legs flying through the deep blue sky. Even a flailing turtle passing by has its legs tangled in a mask. The statistical data of fear is plastered all over the news, the word 'corona' invades our minds hundreds of times a day, and checking both the domestic and the global tally has become a daily habit.

I see tribes in the Amazon forest, who live unconcerned by so-called civilisation, being carried out on stretchers. Rotating the globe, I hear the wailing cries of countless countries: India, Brazil, Indonesia,

Bangladesh....We arrange to meet, then delay and postpone, and now we don't dare make promises. Corona is pulverising cement we had believed to be unbreakable. As we sped ahead singing the New Village movement song 'Better Yourself', as we double- and triple-locked our homes, holing up inside, we didn't realise we'd ended up truly trapped. With growth and progress and development blaring from megaphones, we end up unable to go out to the streets or square or workplace, however much we long to go outside. Steamed hairtail that used to be accompanied by the sound of spoons clashing as they dipped into the same pot, and spicy fish stew that used to be portioned out onto shared platters, now cross the water to reach us. Ordering food which comes through other people's hands and feet, yoked to our shut-up apartments, even our ankle joints creak from want of use, and we can't even go out to the park.

Magnetic Resonance: I can't remember how many times over the course of several months I went inside the machines known as CT and MRI. I entered into barrels, or they moved back and forth, towards me then away. Some rotated of their own accord. I get confused as to whether I was moving inside the machine, or it was moving back and forth. I was lying prone, my chest made to touch a globe-like hole, and they even closed the lid on me. Made to grasp a squishy ball, told to press it if I can't take any more. A single tube was the sole thing connecting me to the outside world. MRI, which bombards the atoms of my body with nuclear magnetic radiance to form a computerised image, from inside the barrel I heard this grating sound. It was like the sound of bone being sawn into. It was as though the sounds of all the things inside my body creaking and crashing into each other, that had so far gone unheard, were being replayed inside me. I was on the point of pressing the ball. While clutching a ball resembling the earth, my lifeline, again and again coming close to giving the call for help, asking them to get me out of this thing, a thought gave me pause. Chagijang, magnetic field. Suddenly chagi meaning magnetic got thought of as chagi meaning self. Is it because of me, that this world I live in is so loud and painful? Have I lived all this time subject to an auditory hallucination, in which what I believed to be the noise of the external world was in fact produced by what is inside me? If so, then isn't the pain of the world because of me? Inside this cacophony, inside the invisible magnetic field of countless branches, I began to ask the question – baby, who are you? To each separate and individual sound pushed out as my every nook and cranny was burrowed into, to the sole and indivisible world that I had mistaken for 'outside', I asked, Baby, baby, what are you really?

Age of rescue: One afternoon around the time when abnormal weather was no longer abnormal, and the depressive state known as the climate crisis had become prominent,

one of my seniors called me. "This is an age of rescue not salvation, an age of the ark, now the rescuer and the rescued are the same, well they say they're in same boat and rescue each other, now there is no time for rescue, in an age of salvation there are people who say we will be saved, and those who do the saving, that's just what you said, what you've been saying your whole life, I've got it, Jesus Confucius Shakyamuni...all the bastards who supposedly were saving humanity, I really envy them, they could say whatever they wanted, tell people to do this and do that, blah blah, an age where we could speak of salvation was so happy, because of course there was hope. That's all over now, that's the reason I drink in the daytime like this and spout a load of nonsense, whatever talk of hope still goes on, the fact is that the world's beyond rescue, in Australia the wildfires are still raging after 6 months, what to do about this fire, we can't put it out. Say Jesus were to come, say Buddha were to come, still not a single one of them can save us..."

Oils poured into concrete and steel frames, felled trees have all become a powder keg, and now the forests are burning. The Alpine glaciers are breaking up, the Himalayan ceiling is breaking apart, and I see Siberia burning in front of my eyes. The Antarctic glaciers melt away to reveal their layers of red inner flesh. If friendship and hospitality and reciprocal labour hadn't been tarmacked over, if we'd left newly-sprouted saplings and deep-rooted trees alone, if we hadn't straitjacketed meandering river courses or dug up gold and silver sands, if those who never had to sweat for it hadn't been able to accumulate an increasing string of zeroes...if we hadn't pampered a method of accumulating money that knows neither limits nor pause, then our children would not have been trapped in water and fire. If we hadn't let go the hands of warm work and play, the solidarity and friendliness of arms around each other's shoulders, of dancing Gang-gang-sul-rae. If the moon, that we used to gaze at reflected in a bowl of water while we sent up a prayer, hadn't been reduced to a means of calculating monthly salary, monthly instalments, monthly rent.

Writing poetry and putting out a book, what does it do...the voice on the phone resonates through me. Trees whose roots are not jam packed into the earth wither to death. Progressiveness that is not overlapped in the chest gets uprooted. Activists who do not extend a bridge to the general public are made to surrender. In the march of mad fetishists who cannot see beyond statistics, in the computerised balance sheet known as 'modern civilisation', I question, therefore I am. Military boots constrict the throat. I resist, therefore I exist.

Chanting prone: It frequently occurs to me that poetry pales in comparison to documentaries. No, that no poem is as painful or sad as real lives. When I see people going out on steep waterfall cliffs to catch fish, just in order to scrape a living. When I see people going to gather honey in the mangrove forest, where a tiger could appear at any moment, or descending a rope 50 metres inside a cave. When I see a baby suckling its mother's breast, not knowing that she is dead. While we gobble and bustle and discard, horses and cows and sheep die in a snowstorm, and 12-year-old Puujee and her mum, forced into herding sheep by the crushing wheels of civilisation, are dying with no access to medicine. In Happyland in the Philippines 11 year old Mick jumps up onto a moving truck to scavenge steel construction materials, amid scorn and hostility. Skin torn and bleeding from rusty nails, Francis will die without being able to see his eighth birthday; what on earth can be the use of poetry? In Indonesia, Nadia spends late nights rooting through a mountain of rubbish, picks up rubber scraps and at school lies down and cries that god is unfair, if I complain then god will hate me, she chants; what on earth is this 'god'? Inside a war, inside a tent, on a boat, trapped in a truck, refugees gaze blankly at the burning and cry out to Allah and the Lord God.

Whether this can be considered good luck or bad, I have never seen god. I haven't even caught a glimpse of a god's heel, though I might have invoked their name very often. And so I have long considered neighbours and friends and comrade siblings and grass and trees and cereals and flowers as gods. Since poverty, sadness, hunger, and suffering are tied together as one bundle like a gift set of cookies, poetry is work that makes me think of Nadia and Mick and Francis and Puujee and, at times, to mourn them. It is my way of saying sorry to lips that cannot cry or speak. Yet what I am truly sorry for, the day when overtime was continued in the tent factory, 17-year-old Hyunok and Youngsook who fall asleep as soon as the lunch bell rings, lying prone with their heads by their sewing machines, too exhausted to eat; and Sooni, after two days of working through the night, who got up as soon as the dinner bell rang then promptly collapsed between a jumper and some cotton scraps – that I never saw their faces properly. That I hadn't realised how, on the two Sunday afternoons a month that were their only time off work, they would go to the bookshop to read essays by Shin Talja and poetry by Kang Eungyo, and from these take heart and obtained the strength to pedal their machines again. And that there are countless Hyunoks and Youngsooks and Soonis and Sunaes. If, as I pray for forgiveness, my embarrassed mutterings could be called poetry, I would chant with great and ceaseless effort. Even if there is no hope, even if salvation has gone away across the water, inside this world where rescue has become an everyday necessity – even if I have to bite my lips and only vowels leak out like a groan – I would look today square in the face, at this happyland borne in an ark, and remember and record.

POET'S ESSAY

POET

Avidya 無明:

The operating room I was wheeled into was like the inside of a refrigerator. I lay shivering on the wheeled bed when a youngster who looked to be the doctor opened my mouth and began counting. Do you know how many teeth you have? No, I don't. He tells me how many. And one, no, two of them wobble; did you know that? No, I didn't. When the anaesthetic wears off and you wake up, if you bite down hard on this respirator, wobbly teeth can fall out. Life seemed like a string of trivial jokes. The doctor casually going on about teeth, while telling me that it's possible I won't wake up from the anaesthetic. With everything else going on, surely he can't think I'd demand compensation for any broken teeth? I take pity on him, doing things by the book. Seen through the windows of the operating room, the sky was bright with floating clouds, like something not of this world. It only took one shot of anaesthetic for me to disappear. Time vanished in one big lump.

I did wake up, but rebellion broke out in regions of my body that were unconnected to the operation. My blood pressure rose severely, a headache spread, and my heart began to race as though it was going to jump out of my chest. When it didn't subside even after taking an antihypertensive and a painkiller, I became a patient requiring special attention. The nurse came each hour to take my measurements, then this got reduced to every 30 minutes. You absolutely have to relax. I became a problem patient, not heeding the nurse's words when she told me to lie down. I wasn't able to say that the reason I couldn't lie down was it made my heart rate feel more threatening. I walked the corridor of the 12th floor, where there were more than 50 other patients, attached to drips here and there. Rain was falling outside the windows of the 12th floor corridor of the Artificial Intelligence Hospital whose very name was artificial. Wet cars and motorbikes standing at a red light were like scattered glimpses of the other world. Unable either to sit or lie down, at a time when my heart was pounding, with the sound of the needle going up past 180mmHg of pressure, poetry leaked out of my mouth like a groan. What might lie between birth and death? What can there be? A single line, shorter than the gash opened up on the nail of my little toe by a glass dish that fell from the fridge. If there was an epitaph, it would be the slender line engraved there, not even 1cm in length: - . In this state of anxiety and panic, I saw shimmering at the window a poet who had died some time ago, by falling from a high floor. It seemed that I might let myself fall. Though saying 'myself', it wouldn't be entirely my own decision. A problem patient locked to the 1cm line between life and death, the nurse had to force me back to the bed.

In desperation I closed my eyes, rested my hands calmly on my heart and stomach, and just breathed deeply. As there was nothing else I could do. Suddenly it seemed as though the lights might have brightened; a hand which, though clearly mine, was larger and brighter, gave off an intense heat. The hand moved a few times, it became a furnace exhaling light. My consciousness grew faint and I even went into a trance, so I couldn't open my eyes. Heat grew in my stomach. It also seemed I briefly caught up on the sleep insomnia had robbed me of. I seemed to simply be aware of the link that we call life, that was hidden inside me, and endlessly meshed outside me, without dividing and analysing it, just as, though I couldn't understand the light, everything inside it seemed alive thanks to it.

Who had breathed without resting my whole life so far? Who had pumped my heart without resting? Who had accompanied me until this point? A time of ignorance when I held a funeral for myself, I knew nothing. I was getting erased, and ignorance and darkness were birthing me. I didn't know how much time passed. The nurse shook my shoulder. She took my blood pressure and smiled broadly. Ah, it's gone right down. Something jerked out of me like a sigh of relief. Forgive me, I spoke too much about too few things, about myself. I failed too greatly, towards the countless beings already inside me.

Small Fry

Since my body won't do what I want it to, feeding myself is a struggle. It seems half a day gets filled with preparing things to eat. Because I am in pain, my body reacts instantly to food. Feeling how true it is that human beings are no more than animals, I pause in slicing a tomato and hold the fruit up to the light. Watery seeds are embedded in the peeled flesh, like molars, like little knives. I slice a firm beet and peer at it. Something like a tree's round growth ring describes a concentric circle there. I'm giddy. Slicing a cabbage, I turn it this way and that, examining it closely. The part connected to the roots and the firm mountain ranges rising from the centre are embedded between thin, soft leaves like a candlewick. Slicing a carrot, I look at how its orange colour fades towards the centre, into the pale green gleam of the core. Organisms that have grown into their specific shape, colour, and scent, replicating themselves as themselves. Turning my body, it hurts here, it hurts there, wincing at each, I end up prostrating myself to what I am going to eat. Ah, so what goes in is what comes out. And what goes out is what comes in. Input and output is connected by a single body.

When a bundle of stiff seaweed ears meets the water, the thick ears wriggle. Ears that had been folded in layers open out, seeping sticky sap. Ears that had been folded inwards curl out, and the sea spreads out. Singing a song of salt and slime. The sound of silence collecting the moment I stop and look. Each time an ear opens out, the march of musical notes seeping out, between one note and another, between in-breath and out-breath, there was a wave dash ~ . The breathing of me and you, of all of you ~ wave dash. The sticky sea forms droplets. Seeing it I thought, seaweed ears are roots, no? Ears are roots, fancy that. Seaweed ears that stuck to rocks on the seabed to support their swaying seaweed leaves speak to me as slimy droplets. Telling me, who had become hard of hearing at some point, to open my ears. Surrounded by YouTube and social media that communicates in one direction only, I am listening in real time to the sound of things right in front of me. To the sound of the world that is resuscitating me, as a unique being both matter and spirit.

A box of large anchovies poured out onto newspaper, hundreds of round eyeballs were looking up at me. In the past, when I was trimming anchovies, my young daughter would draw back and ask, Mum, can those eyes see me? The fishy smell of backs split open, heads torn off, insides ripped out. Eyes that stare open in severed heads, eyes that are looking at those eyes, the question once put from a careful distance is now left out. Those wordless things fill up a lunchbox that only held stir-fried kimchi and radish pickle. Those close-mouthed things gave savour to a poor meal of white radish and green onion. Those small silver bodies each become the strong bones of miner, lathe-worker, and farmer, in bent knees, the joints of their fingers grasping pick-axe, welding machine, and hoe. Like fishers who shake out anchovy nets with a soft uh-sha, like delivery workers who leave boxes by doors without a word. Anchovies are journeyfish, ceaselessly journeying. Dancing as one body, they swoop and dart to avoid larger fish. Plantain that sustains itself and also sustains others by feeding them, silk grass that straightens its neck again after getting trodden down, mung bean grass that doesn't draw the eye...nothings, small fry. O fleabane and goosefoot that grow back even after being pulled up, o penniless poetry, you are being born among weeds that stick their heads back in after being pulled up.

Writing is Revolution

"Revolution is never accomplished through literary delusions." "Revolution is not a literary thing." "Literature is the very essence of revolution." "Revolution arises only from literature and it dies the moment literature is lost." "Reading and writing, these are revolution. We came from revolution." These five propositions, both unconventional and antinomic, are words from one person's lips. Sasaki Ataru determines the truth of these words by investigating the large-scale revolutionary processes of world history. He distinguishes between the world before and after the Fukushima nuclear reactor disaster of 3.11. He says that in the world after 3.11, literature and art are impotent. As indeed they have been at certain other points in history, in other spaces and at other times. But the moment we feel that impotence intensely, is the moment we pick up our pens. Feeling that for the sake of future children, and for our own sake, we have to change this world. Just as Jesus never said "Christianity", Luther didn't use the words "Reformation" or "Protestant". He only read, full of doubt, about the laws and sacred scriptures and morality that the world enforces. He read and read, and then ultimately he wrote. That was a revolution, and it brought another revolution with it. Reading and writing, the young Luther is saying that only these can destroy the structure of exploitation that corrals information, and open up closed territory in all fields. Now there appears to be a thick line drawn in history, dividing before and after corona. Where will this mentality of intense impotence, of impotence intensely felt, be written?

Text is like texture. Text is not a document filled with artificial intelligence. Threads of the living world are woven as a body, warp and weft. Literature is not limited to what gets written on paper and computer. Printed on the paper that is this body, this body that experiences, cries, laughs, eats, drinks, loves, that gets depressed and afraid, that sweats with terror, sheds tears, has palpitations, is a capacious song collectively sung. Dancing while singing and exclaiming, with tears and laughter, and every action that tills pretty fields and constructs attractive fences, has to be treated as art. Our writing and art have to dance in unison with the body of this world. Just as silkworms produce silk as thread from their tails, wouldn't living writing be work that gives wings to the world through the warmth from our own bodies? And writing with eyes that regard the hieroglyphs engraved on the world's body – seeing them as sometimes painful, sometimes beautiful – it might be an act which revolutionises self and world.

Am I saying that things are hopeless? No. There is the seed of a genuine hope, which resists false hope. Um, um, um. The breath of the globe is audible, which is like the vibrations of a heart spreading in the air between heaven and earth. Our enemy is not corona. It is not an invisible virus. It is not some disaster. Since we ourselves are what have created all of these things, escaping from them also has no option but to begin here and now. Look at a young, still-growing bamboo plant, which cannot even be recognised next to a bamboo plant that became fully grown in the space of a few years. Look at a young pine tree, sticking its face out next to a full-grown pine. Let's plant trees, seeds of a new heaven and new earth, in the barren ground inside us. Earthworms are also tilling the earth. Seaweed ears are listening to the language of the deep ocean. Moving as one, shoals of anchovies are rotating silver language. Farmers of the furrowed earth, plant language too, alongside seeds. Delivery workers toiling up steep slopes, attach poetry that touches your heart at the speed of light to the wheels of your motorbikes. Poetry that is sold as a product for a certain amount of won is dying, but poetry is gushing out of your hearts now. Labourers who write books with your bodies, write books. Writing can also become a revolution which alters both the world and ourselves. Time that is dragged out by worries and depression and illness, look at the wide open space. Lay language that is like a hard, sharp sickle on the countless blank spaces that stand precisely between one tree and another, one head of rice and another. Words that are planted with love and harvested with love, instill the breathing of words like the rice ear of the future.

Human Being

One afternoon after a light sprinkling of rain, I lay prone like a hoe and dug up the earth. I dug up grass and earth through the night. Earthworms burrowed slender paths alongside me. From over the wall came the sound of laughter. Since the village hall was closed, the gossip mill had moved here. Today it seems like aunty Jeongin has set up a mill in her front yard. That one crouches all day just to make grass grow, the voices ring out, not beyond finding flaws, as laugher rises and spreads in the air, keeping time.

The laughter of girls who were once not in the

world, and at one time were babes in arms, then at another young girls who would have hurried back into the house when called – Jeongin-ah, Inja-ah, Seungbun-ah, Taeyeol-ah, Yeongja-ah, Yeongju-ah, Geumrye-ah. I myself, and the aunties who knock on my door when I am in pain carrying yukkaejang with taro and sticky rice, freshly made kimchi and seasoned vegetables, were merely great grass. We each were a twirling leaf on a fluttering gleaming tree. Human being, whose past and present are both in the progressive tense, Being Being Human Being, the tune sounded further away, then closer. Bing, bing, bing... infinite spacetime filled with silence and dug-up earth were surrounding embryos that had just opened their eyes, their curled toes. Around ten ri from this field, there is a hill by a reservoir where people from 70 years ago who were burned during the 6.25 war are testifying to those acute days through their copper hairpins and silver hairpins and small bones. Those aunties' older sisters, and neighbours, and paternal aunts and cousins. Outdated people who once cried and laughed while they dug up the earth and reciprocated labour. Our neighbours and members of the human race, who once lived crouched over the earth, looking up at the sky, depending on soil and water, on the surface of the globe, which is no more than a very small part hollow at the centre.

When I groaned in the middle of the night, those who fetched a cloth to wet my mouth and lave my forehead, who smiled to hide their concern, were people poorer than me. When I was turned out of house and home, those who took me in and put me up were people with nothing much going on. When I was hungry, those who fed me were people who do not read thick books like the Buddhist code or the Bible or a writer's complete works. Those who only deal in small change were superheroes to me. The earth and neighbours and friendship were my masters, their hands and feet were prayers and books and sky, food and poetry. Saplings are shooting up higher every day like the flags of the farmers in 1894, the year of the Kabo reforms. This morning they were there on the jars outside – red chilli leaves, kalopanax shoots, Siberian ginseng, ailanthus shoots, all gathered from the woods. I don't know who had left them there. The heavens I don't know will be as many as seeds hidden in manure. I encountered heaven in the course of my life, leaving nothing more to seek. I will live this life then leave it not as poet so-and-so, but exhaling the human being lodged inside me and breathing in organisms that spread limitlessly outside me. Together with the proper names Mi-oak, Mihye, Hyunmi, Misun, Mihee, Misook, Sunhee. Even though extinction and extermination are not far off, I am merely human, there is no need to fly off anywhere. I am merely a mighty commoner, I live as a human being and as a human being I will die.

WHAT THEY SAY ABOUT KIM HAE-JA

POET

For Kim Haeja, love is not something like morals or dogma. It is simply an impulse. Just as people have an impulse for morals and goodness, there is also an impulse for consciousness and an impulse for love. Asking what one thing governs someone more than other things, we can consider them accordingly as a poet, a philosopher, a doctor, a hunter. To put it the other way around, no one is 100% a poet, and no one is 100% a hunter. But there can be an impulse which governs that person overwhelmingly. The impulse that greatly governs Kim Haeja is visible as the love impulse, and that has drawn her unavoidably to the life of a poet. On the other hand, the consciousness impulse modulates the love impulse so that it does not fall into narcissism. Here Kim Haeja's critical intellect is formed.

What makes life tremble with anxiety is when we can feel no certainty. Especially in capitalist society, the anxiety that social norms and national policies will betray us is strong, and makes life wordlessly squalid. And so even more people prefer 'a handful of certainty'. But life is close to "a cart full of beautiful possibility" (Nietzsche, Beyond Good and Evil). Singing and presenting "beautiful possibility", if this is the role and mission of poetry, then Kim Haeja carries it out without fail. That is, while crying, speaking, singing!

Hwang Kyu-kwan, "Without deformity, love is not possible" (The Fortune Teller at Haeja's Place), Walking People, 2018.

Possessed and carnified by others, the poet disappears, and through willingly giving the place of the one who writes poetry to the voice of others, those voices themselves ensure the formation of poetic space. Rather than the poet's subjective emotions and thinking dragging out a story, she gives her voice to the lives of those who live struggling with their whole body, and so the echoes are felt still more strongly. Individual specimens are prominent, but the polyphonic chords and three-dimensional lives constructed by those voices gathered in a single collection are still more moving.

Kim Ki-taek, Literature and Criticism 2018 Autumn

Glimpsed as though in a flash, in Kim Haeja's poems the narrator is possessed like a shaman by various of the people, and the poems unfold through the adept vocalising of their confessions. New poetic innovation and change in ways of thinking arise in scenes where use of dialect and the prosody of spoken language, sensations of the bodies of working people and popular sentiments, all especially vividly felt, overturn the language and ideas of the central intellectual concept of vested rights. I am grateful to encounter an example in which the work of finding the possibility of new language accompanies efforts to coldly confront real life and stand together with the weak.

Han Ki-wook, Literature and Criticism 2018 Autumn

K-POET
HappyLand

Written by Kim Hae-ja | **Translated by** Deborah Smith
Published by ASIA Publishers | 445, Hoedong-gil, Paju-si, Gyeonggi-do, Korea
(Seoul Office: 161-1, Seodal-ro, Dongjak-gu, Seoul, Korea)
Homepage Address www.bookasia.org | **Tel** (822).821.5055 | **Fax** (822) 821.5057
ISBN 979-11-5662-317-5 (set) | 979-11-5662-514-8 (04810)
First published in Korea by ASIA Publishers 2020

This book is published with the support of the Literature Translation Institute of Korea(LTI Korea).

K-픽션 한국 젊은 소설

최근에 발표된 단편소설 중 가장 우수하고 흥미로운 작품을 엄선하여 출간하는 〈K-픽션〉은 한국문학의 생생한 현장을 국내외 독자들과 실시간으로 공유하고자 기획되었습니다. 원작의 재미와 품격을 최대한 살린 〈K-픽션〉 시리즈는 매 계절마다 새로운 작품을 선보입니다.

001 버핏과의 저녁 식사-박민규 Dinner with Buffett-Park Min-gyu
002 아르판-박형서 Arpan-Park hyoung su
003 애드벌룬-손보미 Hot Air Balloon-Son Bo-mi
004 나의 클린트 이스트우드-오한기 My Clint Eastwood-Oh Han-ki
005 이베리아의 전갈-최민우 Dishonored-Choi Min-woo
006 양의 미래-황정은 Kong's Garden-Hwang Jung-eun
007 대니-윤이형 Danny-Yun I-hyeong
008 퇴근-천명관 Homecoming-Cheon Myeong-kwan
009 옥화-금희 Ok-hwa-Geum Hee
010 시차-백수린 Time Difference-Baik Sou linne
011 올드 맨 리버-이장욱 Old Man River-Lee Jang-wook
012 권순찬과 착한 사람들-이기호 Kwon Sun-chan and Nice People-Lee Ki ho
013 알바생 자르기-장강명 Fired-Chang Kangmyoung
014 어디로 가고 싶으신가요-김애란 Where Would You Like To Go?-Kim Ae-ran
015 세상에서 가장 비싼 소설-김민정 The World's Most Expensive Novel-Kim Min-jung
016 체스의 모든 것-김금희 Everything About Chess-Kim Keum-hee
017 할로윈-정한아 Halloween-Chung Han-ah
018 그 여름-최은영 The Summer-Choi Eunyoung
019 어느 피씨주의자의 종생기-구병모 The Story of P.C.-Gu Byeong-mo
020 모르는 영역-권여선 An Unknown Realm-Kwon Yeo-sun
021 4월의 눈-손원평 April Snow-Sohn Won-pyung
022 서우-강화길 Seo-u-Kang Hwa-gil
023 가출-조남주 Run Away-Cho Nam-joo
024 연애의 감정학-백영옥 How to Break Up Like a Winner-Baek Young-ok
025 창모-우다영 Chang-mo-Woo Da-young
026 검은 방-정지아 The Black Room-Jeong Ji-a
027 도쿄의 마야-장류진 Maya in Tokyo-Jang Ryu-jin

Through literature, you
bilingual Edition Modern

ASIA Publishers' carefully selected

Set 1

Division
Industrialization
Women

Set 2
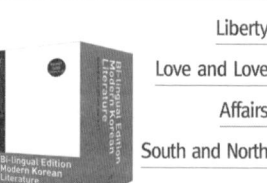

Liberty
Love and Love
Affairs
South and North

Set 3

Seoul
Tradition
Avant-Garde

Set 4

Diaspora
Family
Humor

Search "bilingual edition

can meet the real Korea!
Korean Literature

22 keywords to understand Korean literature

Set 5

Relationships

Discovering

Everyday Life

Taboo and Desire

Set 6

Fate

Aesthetic Priests

The Naked in the Colony

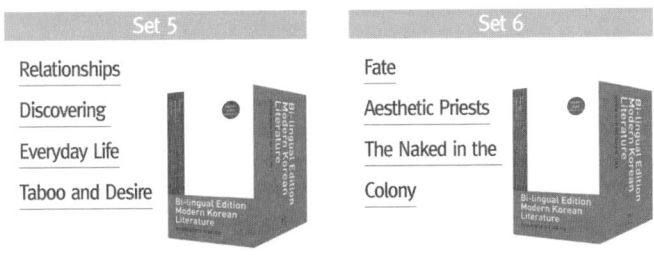

Set 7

Colonial Intellectuals Turned "Idiots"

Traditional Korea's Lost Faces

Before and After Liberation

Korea After the Korean War

korean literature"on Amazon!